The most important thing in life is to h[...] Christ. And the most important part of that [...] munion with Him. He lives in our heart. He speaks to us by [...] and varied ways. Throughout the 6,000 years of Judaic Christian history, many men and women have learned to listen to, to discern and to obey the voice of the Master.

The fundamental thing in the life of Moses was to hear the voice of God. God spoke to Moses, "face to face as one man speaks to another" (Num 12:6-8). Jesus said of Himself, "He only did what the Father told Him" (Jn 5:32). Mary, His mother, was she "who has believed that what the Lord has said to her will be accomplished!" (Lk 1:45). All the saints have learned to hear and obey the voice of the Lord.

Prayer is not simply talking to God; rather, it is a two-way street, a communication between God and us. We must learn to talk and to listen. We must learn the ways in which God speaks to us and what His voice sounds like. Some years ago, someone asked Catherine of Sienna, Why is this that in the Bible God is speaking all over the place, whereas today, hardly anyone hears God." And Catherine said in response, "Because then their prayer was 'Speak Lord, your servant is listening.' Whereas today, our prayer is, 'Listen Lord, your servant is speaking.'"

We who live in such a noisy world must learn to quiet our minds and hearts so that we may listen to, discern and obey the voice of the Lord, not only happiness in this life depends upon it, but also in the next.

Let us pray:

O Heavenly Father,
You who have taught all of your saints to hear your voice,
Teach us how to be still and how to listen.
Teach us what your voice sounds like.
And teach us to obey
So that we may live in your Kingdom
In the name of Jesus, we pray.   Amen.

This is a dynamic, practical, simple book on how to listen to the voice of the Lord. That, after all, is the most often repeated message of the Bible – over 20,000 times God speaks to men and women in the Scriptures. Some of the words that God spoke to men and women like you and me were the following:

To Adam, He said: "You are free to eat from any tree in the garden..." (Gen 2:16)

To Eve, He questioned: "What is this you have done?" (Gen 2:16)

To Noah, He directed: "So make yourself an ark of cypress wood" (Gen 6:14).

To Abram, He instructed: "Leave your country, your people and go to the land I will show you." (Gen 12:1)

AN EXCITING AND REVOLUTIONARY EXPERIENCE

Most people do not realize that God personally is speaking to them all the time. One does not have to be a mystic or a saint to hear the voice of God. The God who lives in our heart communicates with each of us in many and varied ways. To hear and obey the voice of the Lord will revolutionize a person's life. Listening Prayer brings not only wisdom, but also love and power. The spirit of God enlightens our minds with the very thoughts of God, inflames our heart with the very love of God and empowers our life with the very energy of God.

Listening to God is also the most important thing we are asked by God to do – to listen to, discern and obey His voice. Jesus says, "My sheep hear my voice." (Jn 10:27) He promises that if we listen to His voice, many things will happen:

Christ promises that "If you abide in me, and listen to My Word," then:

Your every prayer will be answered. Jesus says, "If you listen to my word, you can ask for anything you wish and you shall have it." If I learn to listen to and discern and obey the voice of the Lord, more and more of my prayers will be answered ... If I always listen and obey, Jesus said they will all be answered. We do not come into this all at once. We go from a "sometimes yes" to a "more so yes" to a "forever yes." There is a poem concerning those who live within the inner circle of "forever yes."

> *There is only one way to find God,*
> *and that is by prayer.*
> *-- Sr. Teresa of Avila*

God's Best

God saves His best things for the few who dare to stand the test.
He has to give his second choice to those who do not really want His best.
It is not always open ill, that risk the promised rest.

Our better often is the foe, that keeps us from God's best.
Sometimes I take the highest choice
Then by trials pressed
I shrink, I yield, I shun the cross
And thus I lose God's best.

So give us today O Lord, Your highest choice
Let the others take the rest
Their good things have no charm for us
We want Your very best
And to Your best we now say "Yes!"

You will become My disciples and experience the fruits of the Holy Spirit.

Jesus says, "In this way you will become my disciples." There are three things that every one of us does all day long no matter whether we are sinner or saint, pagan or Christian. We worship, we love and we disciple that which we worship and love. The woman who is into the soaps, loves the soaps and spends most of her time and energy in front of the television set watching them. And what does she talk about? Obviously, the soaps.

The young man who is into motorcycles, loves motorcycles. And what does he talk about? Motorcycles. The person who is into Jesus, loves Jesus and disciples Jesus. Jesus said, "If you abide in Me and listen to My Word, you will become My disciples." This follows as night follows the day, the God we are into will be the God that we love and the God who we worship and love will be the God who we proclaim in our words.

The fruits of being a disciple of the Lord are love, joy, peace, patience, gentleness, kindness and self-control.

Every day you will have the conviction that I love you, as My Father loves Me.

Jesus says, "I really and truly love you just as much as the Father loves me." Jesus can only love one hundred percent, that is, with all His mind and heart. And the Father loves Jesus with all of His mind and heart. This is an amazing realization that I am loved by Jesus just as much as Jesus is loved by His Father. If you close your eyes, often you will hear Him say, "I love you. Yes, it is you that I love. You are precious in my eyes, and honored. Be not afraid; I am always with you because I love you."

You will have perfect joy even in the midst of your trials and temptations.

Jesus said, "The reason that I'm saying all of this to you is that my joy may be in you, and that your joy may be perfect." Jesus promises us perfect peace and joy in the midst of our trials. Corrie Ten Boom who was portrayed in the move, "The Hiding Place," had a poem that said. "If you look within, you will be depressed. If you look about, you will be distressed. So look at Jesus and be at rest." The more we focus on Christ, the more peace and joy will be in our hearts.

You will be able to love one another with the overflow of that love, which is not human love, but is My love.

Jesus says, "Love one another as I have loved you. The greatest love a man can have for his friends is to lay down his life for them." There is a special love that is THE gift of the Holy Spirit. It is the very love of Jesus in our hearts enabling us to have the length, the breadth and the height and the depth of His marvelous love. The height of this love is that it comes from God. The more we are in to Him, the more He, who is love, is in us. The depth of this love is that it loves the unlovable, forgives the unforgivable, reaches the unreachable, and touches the untouchable. It loves the beggar, the drug addict, the criminal. The breadth of this love is that it loves everyone you meet and the length of this love is that it keeps on loving no matter what. There is no end to it. It is Christ and His Spirit loving others in us and through us.

You will not be strangers but intimate friends whom I will tell where to go, what to do, and what to say.

Jesus says, "I have not called you to be strangers, for a stranger does not know what the Master is about. I called you to be friends because I tell you everything that I hear from My Father." This will be the brunt of this small book. We are not to be strangers who do not hear the voice of the Lord, but God's intimate friends to whom He tells everything.

I will choose you in a ministry of love so powerful that every single thing you ask the Father in My Name, He will give to you. (cf Jn 15:5-25)

Jesus says, "You have not chosen me, I have chosen you; and I appoint you now to bear much fruit so that the Father will give you everything you ask in my name." Each one of us has a divine call upon our lives to continue across our time and our space the redemptive healing, loving work of Jesus. It is the Spirit of Christ working in us and through us, empowering us to reach out to one another. In the line of this ministry, God wants to give to us everything we ask in the name of Jesus. So ask and you shall receive.

It is therefore most important that we hear God speak to us.

"Speak, Lord, for your servant is listening. Incline my heart to Your words, and let your speech come upon me as dew upon the grass."

-- *Thomas 'a Kempis*

"Oh, if souls would only want to listen to My voice when I am speaking in the depths of their hearts, they would reach the peak of holiness in a short time."

-- *Diary of Sister Faustina* (584)

To abide in Christ and hear His voice, we must learn to put Christ in EVERYTHING (cf Jn 15:5-25):

• Give to Jesus the first part of every day
• Go to Him first with every decision.
• Go to Him first with every problem, worry, fear, sin, and weakness.
• Give Him the first place in your heart.
• Give Him the last part of every day.

WAYS THAT GOD SPEAKS

How does God speak? God speaks externally and internally. Externally, He speaks through creation (a sunset, flowers, the ocean), signs and symbols, sacraments, nature, science, people, events, circumstances, books, The Church, the Bible, the Pope, bishops, priests, the lives of the saints, through husbands, wives, children and even through our failures.

Internally, God speaks primarily through our own thoughts, but also through our deepest desires, our intuitions and insights, our dreams, and our visions.

"If you really want to know what God wants you to do, simply ask Him. Make sure you really expect a solid answer for a doubled-minded person will be unsettled as a wave in the sea." (James 1:5-6)

"Now we believe, because we heard for ourselves" (Jn 4:42). God speaks "in many and diverse ways." Let me list some of the most usual ones by first discussing some of the internal ways.

INTERNAL WAYS:

THROUGH OUR THOUGHTS

God's normal interior way of speaking to His children is through their own thoughts, which His Spirit from within puts into their minds. This happens so "naturally" that most of the time, His children miss the realization that the "insights" or thoughts that come to them come from Him. In fact, the first wave of the gifts of the Spirit are "thought" gifts, i.e. wisdom, understanding, knowledge, prophecy, "conscience" and discernment. Wisdom is an overall understanding of God's character and plan. Christian wisdom would mean understanding the basic "kerygma" or the "essential truths" of the gospels.

1. That God as Father has revealed Himself and His Will in many ways to His children.

2. That Jesus as the full revelation of the Father has come into our world to help us think, love and act like Him.

3. That the Spirit of the Father and the Son has been poured forth bringing both gifts and fruits.

4. That together with one another, we form God's covenanted family on earth.

5. That each of us is called to this shared life with Him and one another.

Christian understanding means that we perceive the inter-connection of these truths with life. Christian knowledge, (in Hebrew "to be intimate with") means we have made this our own. Christian prophecy means that we are open to the ongoing "voice" of the Lord. Christian conscience "is discernment". Paul prays, "May the eyes of your understanding be enlightened, and may you have a renewal of your minds so that you may know God's will, what is good, what is acceptable, and what is perfect." (cf Eph 1:17 & Rom 12:1-2)

THROUGH OUR HEARTS

God's next most popular interior way of "speaking" is through the "impressions" He makes upon our hearts. When we realize that God has placed His Spirit "within" us to enlighten our minds and inflame our hearts to do His will, we begin to trust the "impulses of His Spirit" within. So we can say that the second wave of the gifts of the Spirit are "heart" gifts such as love, compassion, sensitivity, caring, longing, awaiting, mercy, zeal, and purity. He sensitizes us; and He expands our ability to face the whole spectrum of human emotions from ecstasy to deep empathy, and from exquisite joy to profound sorrow.

THROUGH DREAMS

A third interior way of God speaking is through dreams. God spoke through dreams frequently in both the Old and New Testaments. Thanks to men like Morton Kelsey and Louis Savage, more and more Christians are open to the power of dreams. Since about one-third of our lives are spent sleeping, let us claim the promise of the Lord, "The Lord gives to His beloved while they sleep" (Ps 127).

THROUGH VISIONS

The fourth internal way of God speaking is through visions. Some people "see" images of God, Jesus and Mary, a loved one or an event. The difference between a vision and an apparition is that a vision is seen interiorly through the "mind's eye" while an apparition is seen through our natural eyes. The difference between a dream and a vision is that a vision is perceived while awake.

THROUGH WEAKNESS AND SIN

Finally, God can speak to us through weaknesses and sins. I used to think that my strengths were my virtues and my weaknesses were my liabilities. I have since changed my mind. My weaknesses have been the source of great graces. They force me to my knees. They humble me and make me compassionate. They help me understand both the awesome love and mercy of God. My "virtues" to the contrary, still are the places where I control, where I do not "sense" my need or vulnerability. With St. Paul, I now pray, "Gladly will I glory in my weaknesses, for in them I am made strong. I can do all things through Christ who strengthens me."

EXTERNAL WAYS:

THROUGH THE CHURCH

God speaks powerfully and clearly through the Church, which He has left behind as the Body of Christ (1 Cor. 12), "The pillar and standard of truth" (1 Tim 3:15). Jesus gave to Peter (Mt 16:18) the keys of binding and loosing and to the apostles the authority to speak in His name. "He who hears you hears Me." Pope John Paul II, His vicar on earth, is speaking so clearly and precisely about God's direction for our lives. His eleven encyclicals, his present cathechesis on the Church (his Wednesday audiences), his almost daily allocutions are hard-hitting, gentle and precise. He is the voice "extraordinare" of Christ on earth.

THROUGH THE NEW CATECHISM

Christ speaks clearly and precisely through the New Catechism of the Church (CCC), which is a "sure and authentic norm" of 1) truth, 2) liturgy, 3) holiness and 4) prayer. I have written a summary of this (124 pages) entitled "A Walk Through the New Catechism."

Obviously, God always speaks primarily through Jesus and Spirit. All of the above are remote causes, that is secondary instruments. In all revelation, Jesus and the Spirit are at work.

THROUGH OTHERS

God's primary way of "speaking" to those inexperienced in listening to Him for themselves is through others, usually those placed "over" them such as parents, pastors, teachers, guardians, and so forth. As a person develops, however, internal evidence becomes more important than external. In fact, since Vatican II, millions of people have shifted their antennae from exterior to primarily interior "voices" or thoughts and impressions received in prayer. This was brought about primarily through the renewal moments such as the Charismatic, Cursillo, House of Prayer, Catechetical, Foculare, Directed Retreat and Renew movements. God's spokespersons can be anyone, even a child or a very simple person.

THROUGH THE WORD

The Bible is the "inspired" external word of God for all men and women. In His Word is wisdom for the ages. The scriptures are thus normative for Christian living. Christ's mind, heart, principles, character and plan are essentially therein revealed. It is, however, not so much a prescription like an "owner's manual" as it is a "description" of the type of relationship men and women today are having with the living God. Sometimes God will lead us over and again to the same passage, often with deeper and different insights. Through His Word, God inspires us, enlightens us, comforts us, challenges us, fills us, heals us, warns us, assures us, expands us, and sends us.

THROUGH SIGNS AND SYMBOLS

A fifth way that God speaks exteriorly is through symbols such as a burning bush, a hug, a kiss, a bent knee, a bowed neck. In her marvelous book, "Every Bush Is Burning", Sister Joan Puls, O.S.F., says that "more and more people need to see the connection between ordinary reality and divine faith." For in the words of Gerald Mauley Hopkins, "The world is charged with the grandeur of God." Everything can point beyond itself and thus become a sign of sacrament of not only water and oil and raised hands, but also trees, sun, sky, and sea. Father Richard Rohr has made many of us realize the power of the "non-rational". In our Western world of abstraction, we need the artists and poets to assume their prophetic role. They keep our "spirituality" incarnational and "enfleshed," therefore truly Christian.

Although every Christian can be given the gift of prophecy (cf 1 Cor 14), and although Moses prayed, "Would that everyone were a prophet," true prophets are rare. Still, the Church, at any time, is built upon them as foundations (cf Eph 2:20). Our age needs them desperately. So God gives them in many like Mother Teresa of Calcutta, in priests like Daniel Berrigan and Rick Thomas, in popes like John XXIII, in bishops like Thomas Gumbleton and Robert Moreau, in lay women like Dorothy Day, in laymen like Charles Colson, and in ministers like Bill Gothard and Dave Wilkerson.

They always take us to the cutting edge of life where the Gospel, in its simplicity and power, meet the world in its complexity and weakness. They take us beyond where we wish to go. So often, we persecute them rather than listen to them. They are men and women who preach by the way they live more than by the words they say.

THROUGH CIRCUMSTANCES

Another way of the Lord speaking is through circumstances. God being God controls everything. There are no co-incidences; there are only "God-incidences". Everything is working out for the good, for those who love God – everything (cf Rom 8:28). Once God opens a door, no man can close it. Once He closes a door, no man can open it. (Rev 3:8; Is 22:22).

THROUGH PARABLE AND PARADOX

Another way that God speaks a disarming word to us is through parable and paradox. We, in our unconscious desire to stay in control, want nicely wrapped religious concepts. But God's ways are not our ways. Most times, they are just the opposite. The first will be last, the rich will be poor, the slave will be master, the old shall be young, the lion shall be gentle, the flowers will bloom in the steep, the rivers shall flow in the desert, the rough ways made plain.

The impossible with God and the Kingdom of God shall reign on earth. The basic problem with so much fundamentalism is that it misses the obvious – God is bigger than our boxes and brighter than our mysteries. Sufferings turn into joy and light shines in darkness. If you think you understand, you probably don't; and if you are searching, you most likely will find. Only those who "stand under" Jesus, understand the parabolic and paradoxical nature of His character and message. The wise person is able to rest with mystery and paradox. The Catholic answers most are "both/and" rather than "either/or".

THROUGH WISE COUNSEL

God speaks always through wise counsel, be it in the form of a wise spiritual director or a friend in the Lord. He wants us to see and listen to the "Spirit" in one another. No man is an island. There are no "Lone Rangers" in His Kingdom. People need the Lord and they need one another. He wants to give us anointed leadership.

THROUGH PAIN AND SUFFERING

A deep and profound way that God speaks is through our "crosses," that is through the pain we all experience be it physical, emotional or spiritual. Nothing so "breaks" us as sadness, loneliness, despair, sickness, alienation and separateness. Broken hearts are the vehicle of grace. No one is spared. We hold the treasure of grace in clay pots, as Paul says; or as others say, in "cracked pots". We are all "psycho-ceramics"; yet it is precisely through the "cracks" that God's love shines and the oil of the Spirit leaks out. Our wounds are our glory. They remind us of our desperate need. They humble us and we learn more in the valleys than on the mountain tops. More through suffering and defeat than through victory and success. God calls us to faithfulness more than success.

THREE WAYS OF LISTENING TO THE VOICE OF CHRIST IN PRAYER

I. PRAYING THE SCRIPTURES UNDER THE ANOINTING OF THE SPIRIT

In John 5:39, Jesus says to the scribes of His day, "You search the Scriptures thinking that in them you will find life and they reveal ME AND YOU REFUSE TO COME TO ME TO FIND LIFE." He is teaching them and us that the

Scriptures, especially the New Testament, must be read with His Spirit opening our eyes to their real meaning. In Luke 24, as Jesus talks with His disciples on the road to Emmaus – "beginning with Moses and the prophets" – He opened their eyes to all the Scriptures taught "concerning Himself."

The disciples response was "were not our hearts burning inside us as He walked with us along the way and opened the Scriptures to us."

This is what Jesus wants to do for each of us – to open the personal, here and now, tailor-made meaning of His Word to us.

We must therefore, only read the Scriptures under the anointing of His Spirit. To read the Bible with our eyes will only blind us to their real meaning and divide the Church. Behold, today we have well over 4,000 different Protestant denominations, each calling themselves His followers yet each turning from the true Church He founded that day in Caesarea Philippi when He said to Peter, "You are Peter, and upon this rock I will build MY Church" (Mt 16:18).

There is only one Church – so the Scriptures must be read in the context of that Church and her teachings and under the anointing of His Spirit. If so, they will be understood – "in Christ."

A Simple Method

Place – Find yourself a quiet place where you can be alone with Christ as you read His Word.

Presence – Put yourself in the presence of Christ by:

1) Saying an Act of Consecration to Him – "Lord, I am totally yours. Speak, your servant is listening."

2) Reciting an Act of Contrition to cleanse your soul of all sins and unforgiveness.

Passage – Ask the Holy Spirit to put into your thoughts a page number or a passage from the Scriptures, preferably the New Testament. "Ask and you will receive." Something will come to you as you ask. Then turn to that page or passage.

Point or Principle – As you read the passage, something will impress you. Some say certain words appear as if "in gold" or something will "hop off the page" or "touch your heart." You will intuitively get the point. It will be personal and practical, such as "forgive your husband," "go here," "do this," "don't do that," "relax," "forget," "do not worry about that."

Practice – Once you get the personal, practical point or principle, put it into action. Practice it. If Jesus told you to forgive someone, then forgive him. If He told you to do something, do it. The wise man who built his house upon the rock is he who hears the word of the Lord and obeys it" (Mt 7).

II. KEEPING A SPIRITUAL JOURNAL

Another concrete way of hearing God is to go apart and listen as God speaks to you through your own thoughts, then writing them down. It is today called "journaling", but this method has been around for 6,000 years. The first one to keep a journal was Moses. We have five of his journals. We call them the Books of Moses (the first five books of the Bible.) The Bible (literally) itself is a collection of 72 journals. 72 sacred authors wrote down the inspirations of the Holy Spirit. Therefore, we say that God is the primary author and the sacred writer (Matthew, Luke or John) is the secondary author.

A Simple Method of Journaling

Six keys to journaling are:

KEY ONE: Quiet yourself. Go off by yourself to a quiet place, sit in a comfortable chair and pray to the Holy Spirit to QUIET your mind of all the "marketplace" thoughts (i.e., the worldly, egoistic, worrying, negative thoughts that tend to fill it).

KEY TWO: Focus on Jesus. Try to picture Jesus (if you are imaginative and intuitive) or think of the word "Jesus" over and over again until your mind is absorbed in Him. When you are absorbed in Him, ask Him to speak to you through your thoughts or intuitions.

KEY THREE: Be now aware of the flow of spontaneous thoughts that come into your mind. They just seem to bubble up from within.

KEY FOUR: Write down in a journal these messages you are receiving in a flow of spontaneous writing (i.e., these thoughts that are bubbling forth). Have faith that God is answering your prayer. You have asked, now receive in faith.

KEY FIVE: Sort out or discern with Scripture or another spiritual person the messages you are receiving to see if it is from the Holy Spirit, from you or an evil source. Follow the principles of discernment. (See the next section.)

KEY SIX: Once you are relatively certain (remember, it's a faith journey) that something you received is of God, step out in faith and do it.

"The wise man who built his house upon the rock is he who listened to the Word of the Lord and obeyed it" (Mt. 7).

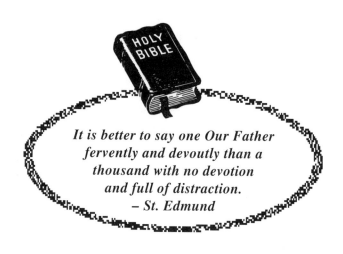

It is better to say one Our Father fervently and devoutly than a thousand with no devotion and full of distraction.
– St. Edmund

III. PRAYING THE OUR FATHER

One of Jesus' disciples said to Him, "Lord, teach us to pray as John taught his disciples" (Lk 11:1). Jesus answered, "AFTER THIS MANNER PRAY ... Our Father Who Art in Heaven, Hallowed Be Thy Name, ... etc." Now each of you is thinking, hey, I say the "Our Father". I even know it by heart. But that's the problem. We say the "Our Father"; we don't pray the "Our Father".

Using the wealth of our Spiritual tradition, let us go through the five principles of the Our Father one by one and really pray. The use of these principles can transform us into "other Christs," can transform our daily pray time from a chore into a delight.

The first part of the prayer concerns God, His Kingdom, His Will, His Providence. The second part concerns us and our needs.

FIRST PRINCIPLE:
PRAISE "HALLOWED BE THY NAME"

The first thing that Jesus taught us was PRAISE: "Our Father, hallowed be Thy name." Praising God takes us out of self and puts us into God. Spirituality is not so much inviting God into our little and picayune hearts as it is accepting God's invitation to come up into His heart that has a length, breath, height and depth that is beyond anything we can think of or imagine. Praise frees up everything within us. When we praise God, such as by saying:

> "Oh God, you are
> so holy – all holy
> so wonderful – all wonderful
> so loving – all loving
> so merciful – all merciful
> so majestic – all majestic
> so powerful – all powerful

then we forget ourselves. As the song goes, "So forget about yourself and concentrate on Him and worship Him."

Whenever St. Theresa, the Little Flower, got bogged down with her problems and would cry out to the Father, He would take her in Spirit into His loving arms and from this high vantage point she would look down on her now little problems and wonder how she ever could have worried about them at all. Praise links us to God, not to ego. Praise stirs up the Spirit within us. Praise lifts us out of selfishness, worry and fear. Praise can lead us spiritually, emotionally, and even physically (away from ourselves).

I Have Only Today

My life is an instant,
An hour which passes by;
My life is a moment
Which I have no power to stay;
You know, O my God,
That to love You here on earth –
I have only today

-- Therese of Lisieux

"Our thoughts in this present life should turn on the praise of God, because it is in praising God that we shall rejoice forever in the life to come; and no one can be ready for the next life unless he trains himself for it now.

We are praising God now, assembled as we are here in church; but when we go our various ways again, it seems as if we cease to praise God. But provided we do not cease to live a good life, we shall always be praising God. You cease to praise God only when you swerve from justice and from what is pleasing to God. If you never turn aside from the good life, your tongue may be silent but your actions will cry aloud, and God will perceive your intentions; for as our ears hear each other's voices, so do God's ears hear our thoughts."

-- St. Augustine on Praise

We praise God as Our Father. What a beautiful realization that the God who made the heavens and earth wishes to be called "Our Father". So we can worship Him as Father – the one who gives life, the one who loves us unconditionally, the one who is covenanted to provide for our needs, the one who feeds us and protects us, our Abba (cf Ps 91:12; Isa. 32:1, 41:1-3; Ps. 23: 1-4; Ps. 100; Ps. 36; Ps. 145).

Praise God As Our Father, Our Abba

The most celebrated picture of this is found in Luke (15:11-32), in the story of the father of the prodigal son, who is never more of a father than when he welcomes home (back into the family) the one who by his words and deeds has brought shame

upon himself and has caused sorrow and pain to those who truly love him. This phrase "Our Father" not only introduces the prayer, but it is also the dominant theme of it.

ABBA PRAYER

> *Abba, I adore you.*
> *Abba, I adore you.*
> *Abba, I adore you.*
> *Abba, my Abba.*

(Continue this gentle repetition until you sense completion of the prayer work.)

As Father, God is a living, thinking, loving Being (cf. Acts 17:24-29; 1 Tim 6:15-16; 1 Tim 1:17). He is more than just a divine Mind, or Creator, or First Cause; He is a loving, caring Father. Praising Him opens our spirits to all that He has in store for us.

A PRAYER OF AWE

> *You, O eternal Trinity, are a deep sea into which,*
> *the more I enter, the more I find, and the more I find,*
> *the more I seek.*
> > *O abyss,*
> > > *O eternal Godhead,*
> > > *O sea profound,*
> *what more could You give me than yourself?*
> > *Amen.*

-- *Catherine of Siena*

So the first part of our prayer time should be a time of PRAISE. Praise opens the floodgates of the Father's love and mercy. Read quietly or aloud the following litany of praise and allow it to open your spirit and draw you into the realm of the miraculous and into the abundant life in which God created us to live. Add praises of your own!

Litany of Praise to Jesus

Praise You, Jesus, You are my Life, my Love.
Praise You, Jesus, You are the Name above all names.
Praise You, Jesus, You are the King of creation.
Praise You, Jesus, You are the King of the universe.

Praise You, Jesus, You are the Lord of lords.
Praise You, Jesus, You are the Almighty.
Praise You, Jesus, You are Christ, the King.
Praise You, Jesus, You are the Lamb of God.
Praise You, Jesus, You are the Bright Morning Star.
Praise You, Jesus, You are our Champion and Strength.
Praise You, Jesus, You are the Way for our life.
Praise You, Jesus, You are the only Truth.
Praise You, Jesus, You are the Wonderful Counselor.
Praise You, Jesus, You are the Prince of Peace.
Praise You, Jesus, You are the Light of the World.
Praise You, Jesus, You are the Living Word.
Praise You, Jesus, You are our Redeemer.
Praise You, Jesus, You are the Messiah.
Praise You, Jesus, You are the Anointed One.
Praise You, Jesus, You are the Good Shepherd.
Praise You, Jesus, You are the Lord of hosts.
Praise You, Jesus, You are the Rock of all ages.
Praise You, Jesus, You are the Savior of the World.
Praise You, Jesus, You are the Bread of Life.
Praise You, Jesus, You are the Font of all holiness.
Praise You, Jesus, You are the Living Water.
Praise You, Jesus, You are the True Vine.
Praise You, Jesus, You are my Spouse, my Maker.
Praise You, Jesus, You are our Fortress.
Praise You, Jesus, You are the Deliverer.
Praise You, Jesus, You are our Victory.
Praise You, Jesus, You are our Salvation.
Praise You, Jesus, You are our Wisdom.
Praise You, Jesus, You are our Sanctification.
Praise You, Jesus, You are the great I AM.
Praise You, Jesus, You are the great High Priest.
Praise You, Jesus, You are our Joy.
Praise You, Jesus, You are my Healing and Wholeness.
Praise You, Jesus, You are our Covenant.
Praise You, Jesus, You are the Most High God.

Praise You, Jesus, You are the Just Judge.

Praise You, Jesus, You are my Defense.

Praise You, Jesus, You are my Protector.

Praise You, Jesus, You are my Provider.

Praise You, Jesus, You are the Bridegroom.

Praise You, Jesus, You are my Patience.

Praise You, Jesus, You are the Resurrection and the Life.

Praise You, Jesus, You are the Alpha and the Omega.

Praise You, Jesus, You are all that I need.

Praise You, Jesus, You are all that I want.

Praise You, Jesus, You are worthy of all praise!

SECOND PRINCIPLE:
PLAN "THY KINGDOM COME, THY WILL BE DONE"

This marvelous Father-God, whom we honor, praise and worship, has a plan for our lives that He reveals step-by-step and moment-by-moment, both individually and collectively. God's plan was to send Jesus into the world and into our hearts, enabling us to think, love and act like Jesus. And the Power to do that (the Holy Spirit) has been poured into us giving us, through the wisdom, heart and power, gifts of the Holy Spirit. Therefore, God wants us to ask Him to reveal His Kingdom and His Will.

In James 1:5, it says, "If you really want to know what God wants you to do, simply ask Him and He will gladly tell you." We must believe that God speaks or reveals His plan in such a way that we can hear it and follow it. There are some who believe that God has only revealed the skeletal outline of that plan through the Bible and the teachings of our Church. There are others who believe that revelation ceased with the death of the last apostle.

The insight of this prayer is that God speaks to all His children all the time. We can listen to God as He reveals that part of His inbreaking Kingdom each day and that part of His Will for the moment. Now is the time to quiet our minds and hearts and spend time listening. I would suggest here the first two methods of listening prayer:

1. Praying with Scripture under the anointing
2. Keeping a Spiritual Journal

Prayer is a conversation where we talk to God; but more importantly, it is one during which God talks to us. It is a two-way street during which the One with the greater message should have more time to speak, that is, God.

There are several kinds of prayer – formal prayer, informal prayer, meditative prayer, prayer of anguish, prayer of faith, hope, love, contrition, and contemplative prayer.

Take your example from "people of prayer" in Scripture. Moses, whose face reflected God's glory (cf Ex. 34:33, 35). Mary, who listened and did the will of the Father (Lk 1:26-38). And Jesus, who taught that the message of prayer is that of a life lived abundantly, one that is lived in relationship with the Source of Life, the Father. The essence of Jesus' prayer is Jesus saying "Yes" to the still voice of the Father, doing only what the Father tells Him to do. In short, prayer is learning always to listen to God talking to us.

If we faithfully ask God to speak to us and reveal His Kingdom and His Will, He will! "Ask and you shall receive" is a promise. When we really seek God's Kingdom and Will with all our heart, we will find Him. We can continually flow out of God by listening to His voice spoken in the present moment.

THIRD PRINCIPLE:
PROVISION "GIVE US THIS DAY OUR DAILY BREAD"

God wishes to provide for all our needs. This is the promise of the covenant. This is the lesson of the Exodus journey. Having God as Father, we are rich, no matter what. There in the desert, they had no money, no stores, no doctors, no insurance companies, no banks, no securities. All they had was God and His Providence. This is His promise to us, to provide for all our needs. Thus, God fed them, healed them, helped them, guided them, and clothed them for 40 years.

In a materialistic culture where most of us tend to rely more on money than on God, we need to believe that God wants to provide for our daily needs. So use this time of prayer to present your petitions. DON'T BUY IT, PRAY FOR IT would be a modern interpretation. It really works. GOD PROVIDES. ASK AND YOU SHALL RECEIVE.

Here at My Father's House Retreat Center, we have learned to ask. When we were refurbishing our Chapel, we needed an altar. So we prayed for one. Shortly afterward, Father George from St. Mary's Ukrainian Church in Colchester gave us a beautiful altar. Then we needed pews. Monsignor Normand Methe from St. Mary's in Stamford gave us the pews. On and on it went. God provides. He's more reliable, practical and economical than money. Besides as Jesus tells us, you can't put your faith in God AND money, it's one or the other.

One fourth of the teachings of Jesus teach us to rely more on the Father and less on money. He must have seen how difficult it would be for a materialistic people to get the point. Don't rely on money, rely on My Father to "give you your daily" food, bread, shoes, transportation, rent, clothing, and so forth. Look up at the birds. It works. Look at the flowers. It works. Look at Him. It works.

> "Therefore I tell you, do not worry about your life, what you will eat or drink; or about your body, what you will wear. Is not life more important than food, and the body more important than clothes? Look at the birds of the air; they do not sow or reap or store away in barns and yet your heavenly Father feeds them. Are you not much more valuable than they? Who of you by worrying can add a single hour to his life? And why do you worry about clothes? See how the lilies of the field grow. They do not labor or spin" (Mt 6:25-28).

As these verses from Matthew tell us, nothing is more important in our spiritual life than to say "Yes" to Jesus with all our heart and soul, and then to let the Holy Spirit work out its meaning in our life. God loves us without measure and will always be with us, protecting us and guiding us. The more we open up, yield and simply allow ourselves to be drawn deeply into the Lord's love, the more our lives will be directed and come into alignment with God's Will.

PRAYER OF SELF-DEDICATION

Lord Jesus Christ, take all my freedom,
My memory, my understanding, and my will.
All that I have and cherish You have given me.
I surrender it all to be guided by Your will.
Your grace and Your love are wealth enough for me.
Give me these, Lord Jesus, and I ask for nothing more.

> *To fall in love with God is the greatest of all romances; to seek Him, the greatest adventure, to find Him, the greatest human achievement.*

Recite the following prayer daily and notice the changes it makes in your life as you begin to turn everything over to the Lord and trust in His tender mercy.

A PRAYER OF SURRENDER

"... may Your will be done" (Mt 26:42)

Loving Father,

I surrender to You today with all my heart and soul. Please come into my heart in a deeper way. I say, "Yes, to You today. I open all the secret places of my heart to You and say, "Come on in." Jesus, You are Lord of my whole life. I believe in You and receive You as my Lord and Savior. I hold nothing back.

Holy Spirit, bring me to a deeper conversion to the person of Jesus Christ. I surrender all to You: my time, my treasures, my talents; my health, my family, my resources, my work, relationships, time management, successes and failures. I release it and let it go.

I surrender my understanding of how things ought to be, my choices and my will. I surrender to You the promises I have kept and the promises I have failed to keep. I surrender my weaknesses and strengths to You. I surrender my emotions, my fears, my insecurities, my sexuality. I especially surrender (here mention other areas of surrender as the Holy Spirit reveals them to you.)

Lord, I surrender my entire life to You, the past, the present, and the future. In sickness and in health, in life and in death, I belong to You. (Remain with the Lord in a spirit of silence through your thoughts, a heart song or simply staying in His presence and listening for his voice.)

"Take, Lord, and receive, all my liberty,
my memory, my understanding,
and my whole will.
You have given me all that I have,
all that I am,
and I surrender all to Your Divine will.
Give me only Your love and Your grace.
With this I am rich enough,
and I have no more to ask."

Amen.

--Prayer of St. Ignatius

FOURTH PRINCIPLE:
PERSONAL RELATIONSHIP
"FORGIVE US OUR TRESPASSES AS WE FORGIVE THOSE WHO TRESPASS AGAINST US"

This principle is explosive. Let God forgive you and forgive others. FOR-GIVENESS IS GOD'S ANSWER. It flows from His love and mercy, His "hesed" and "emeth." It's the only real answer.

Even today after the coming of Jesus, most men and women live lives burdened with guilt and with shame. Psychologists have no answer for this. What they do tell us, however, is that most people handle guilt, bitterness, hatred or shame using one or more of four mechanisms: repression, denial, rationalization, and projection. But it doesn't go away.

Jesus, after his horrendous death and glorious resurrection to save us from sin and shame, appeared to the apostles on Easter Sunday evening through closed doors. He said to them, "As the Father has sent me, so do I send you." Then he breathed on them and said, "Receive the Holy Spirit. Whose sins you shall forgive they are forgiven, and whose sins you shall retain, they are held bound."

But as Catholic Christians, we have the only practical, powerful, foolproof answer to guilt, bitterness, hatred and shame, and it is FORGIVENESS through Confession. Because God holds us responsible for every one of our thoughts, words, actions, attitudes and motives, He – in the abundance and richness of His mercy – has given to us in the Sacrament of Reconciliation a way out of these negative emotions.

We used to call it penance, but it really is a sacrament of love, a sacrament that lets us allow Jesus to take away everything that divides and destroys us from living in the presence and loving union with God.

THE SACRAMENT OF RECONCILIATION

There are several steps we can take in making a meaningful confession:

STEP ONE: Examine your conscience – *Don't be hasty – Don't be superficial – Avoid anxiety*

Many of these sins are mortal and the Eucharist is forbidden until a good confession is made to a priest. If in doubt whether a sin is mortal or venial, confess it and consult a good catechism or priest very loyal to the Holy Father and Rome's teachings. A mortal sin involves a serious matter, sufficient reflection takes place and it is committed with full consent of the will.

1. Have I denied or doubted God's existence? Have I refused to believe God's revelation? How often have I broken the first commandment by giving more of my heart to my job, my family, my pleasure, my interests, my finances? How often have I truly worshipped God? How often have I put Him first in my life? Have I doubted or presumed upon God's mercy? Have I neglected prayer for a long time? Have I denied that I was a Catholic? Did I heave the Catholic faith? Have I been involved with ouija boards, horoscopes, tarot cards, fortune tellers, seances, occult religions, Silva Mind Control, EST, Transcendental Meditation, Eastern Religions, etc?

2. Have I taken the Lord's name in vain or blasphemed God or sworn? Have I broken an oath or vow?

3. Have I missed Mass on Sunday or performed unnecessary work on Sunday? Did I really make it the "Lord's Day"? Am I always reverent in the presence of Jesus in the most Blessed Sacrament? Was I inattentive at Mass? Have I come to Mass late or left Mass early?

4. Have I obeyed all lawful authority (parents, boss, police, government, etc.)? Have I neglected my duties to my husband, wife, children or parents? Have I failed to actively take an interest in the religious education and formation of my children? Have I failed to educate myself on the true teachings of the Church? Have I given a full day's work in return for my full day's pay? Have I given a fair wage to my employee?

5. Did I agree that killing is allowable? Am I "Pro-Choice" on the abortion questions? Have I had or consented to an abortion or assisted another in obtaining one? Have I consented to murder in any of its forms? Have I contributed to destructive gossip? Was I impatient, angry, envious, unkind, proud, jealous, revengeful, hateful toward others, lazy? Did I give bad example, abuse drugs, drink alcohol to excess, fight or quarrel?

6. Have I been impure in thought, word or action either along or with another (including promiscuity, homosexuality, adultery, fornication, immortal books, videos, conversations, innuendoes, jokes)? Have I committed adultery against God through spiritual infidelity? Have I given scandal by what I said or did, especially to the young? Was I the cause of anyone leaving the faith?

7. Have I stolen?

8. Have I lied?

9. Have I "desired" another's spouse?

10. Have I been content with my goods? Have I been envious of another? Have I been proud – looking down at others because of race, appearance, ethnic origin, manner of dress, etc.?

PRECEPTS OF THE CHURCH

Have I also attended Mass on Holy Days?
Do I go to confession often?
Do I receive communion often?
Do I respect the laws of the Church concerning marriage?
Do I contribute my time, talent and treasure to my parish?

STEP TWO: Be truly sorry for your sins and make a firm purpose not to sin again.

STEP THREE: Forgive everyone who has ever hurt you or harmed you in any way.

STEP FOUR: Go to confession (i.e., confess your sins to a priest in the beautiful healing Sacrament of Reconciliation, as shown on next page).

Procedure in the Confessional

The priest may begin with a Scripture reading. After he finishes, you say: "Bless me, Father, in this confession. It has been - (state length of time, i.e., # of weeks or months) – since my last confession. I accuse myself of the following sins."

Then tell your mortal sins and the number of times committed. If you have no mortal sins to confess, then confess two or three venial sins you have committed since your last confession. When you have finished telling your sins, you should say:

> *"For these and all the sins of my past life, especially for my sins of – I am truly sorry."*

The priest now gives the necessary advice, assigns your penance and asks you to say the *Act of Contrition* (see below). Then wait and listen as the priest gives the absolution. Then say THANK YOU, FATHER, and leave the Confessional and perform the penance assigned by the priest.

Act of Contrition

> *"Oh my God, I am heartily sorry for having offended Thee, and I detest all my sins, because of Thy just punishment, but most of all because they offend Thee, my God, Who art all good and deserving of all my love. I firmly resolve, with the help of Thy grace, to sin no more and to avoid the near occasions of sin. Amen."*

STEP FIVE: Thank God for His love and mercy (for dying on the Cross that you could be set free from guilt by the Blood of Jesus).

STEP SIX: Do the penance the priest gave you.

The only answer is God's answer – FORGIVENESS. And the only thing that God asks us is to PASS IT ON. FORGIVE OTHERS AS I FORGIVE YOU. So now that we've asked to be forgiven, we need to forgive those against whom we carry buried emotions of anger, bitterness and resentment. Decide to be reconciled with all the people in your life. Set them free and set yourself free in the process. Break the chains of unforgiveness and let go of anything that you hold against another person.

Offer this prayer of forgiveness for 30 days, and release the burdens that you hold deep in your heart.

FORGIVENESS PRAYER

Loving Father,

I choose to forgive everyone in my life, including myself, because You have forgiven me. Thank You, Lord, for this grace. I forgive myself for all my sins, faults and failings, especially *(mention specific failings)*. I forgive myself for not being perfect, I accept myself and make a decision to stop picking on myself and being my own worst enemy. I release the things held against myself, free myself from bondage and make peace with myself today, by the power of the Holy Spirit.

I forgive my MOTHER for any negativity and unlove she may have extended to me throughout my life, knowingly or unknowingly, especially *(mention a specific event or negative behavior)*. For any abuse of any sort, I do forgive her today. For any way that she did not provide a deep, full, satisfying mother's blessing, I do forgive her today. I release her from bondage and make peace with her today.

I forgive my FATHER for any negativity and unlove he may have extended to me throughout my life, knowlingly or unknowingly, especially *(mention a specific event or negative behavior)*. For any and all abuses, unkind acts, hurts, and deprivations I do forgive him today. For any way that I did not receive a full, satisfying father's blessing, I forgive him today. I release him from bondage and make peace with him today.

I forgive my SPOUSE for any negativity and unlove extended throughout our time together, especially *(mention a specific event or negative behavior)*. For all the wounds of our relationship, I do forgive my spouse today. I release my spouse from bondage and make peace between us today.

I forgive my CHILDREN for any hurts, especially *(mention a specific time or behavior)*. I release them from bondage and make peace with them today. Bless them, Lord.

I forgive my SISTERS and BROTHERS for any negativity and unlove, especially *(mention a specific event or negative behavior)*. I forgive my BLOOD RELATIVES for any abuses, especially *(mention)*. I forgive my ANCESTORS for any negative actions that affect my life today and make it harder for me today to live in the freedom of a child of God. I release them from bondage and make peace with them today, in Jesus' name.

I forgive my FRIENDS for any actions of negativity and unlove, especially *(mention a specific event or negative action)*. For any time they abused our relationship or led me astray, I do forgive them. I release them from all bondage and make peace with them today, in the power of the Holy Spirit.

I forgive my EMPLOYERS of the present and the past for any negativity and unlove, especially *(be specific)*. I release them from all bondage and pray a blessing on them today, in Jesus' name.

I forgive all SCHOOL TEACHERS for any negative, abusive actions, especially *(be specific)*. I release them from all bondage and pray a blessing on them today, in Jesus' name.

I forgive all LAWYERS, DOCTORS, NURSES, and other professionals, especially for *(be specific)*.

I forgive CLERGY and all representatives of the Church, especially *(mention)*. I release them all, in Jesus' name.

I forgive every member of SOCIETY who has hurt me in any way; those who have hurt me by criminal action or who have harmed my family, I forgive all in public life who have passed laws opposing Christian values. I forgive all the unfair, anonymous sources of pain and annoyance in my life.

Heavenly Father, I now ask for the grace to forgive the ONE PERSON IN MY LIFE WHO HAS HURT ME THE MOST. The one who is the hardest to forgive, I now choose to forgive, though I may still feel angry and hurt. I also make peace with the one family member, the one friend and the one authority figure who has hurt me the most.

Lord, is there anyone else I need to forgive? *(Be still and listen.)*

Thank You, loving Father, for setting me free.

I now pray a blessing on those who have hurt me. Lord, do something special for each of them today. Thank You, Lord. I praise You. Amen.

FIFTH PRINCIPLE:
POWER/PROTECTION "LEAD US NOT INTO TEMPTATION, BUT DELIVER US FROM EVIL"

God is our Protector. He really is. He warns us of all impending evil: spiritually from sin; emotionally from worldly depression and fear; and physically from any danger. We have to learn how to hear His voice so that we will heed His warnings.

He does not wish that we go crashing into the obstacles in the minefield of life. He warns us of their coming and shows us a way out. The following is a prayer for protection that God will always keep us in His care as loving and devoted Christians.

Dear Lord Jesus, I Need You!

Dear Lord Jesus, I need You. I can't live the Christian life by myself. When I try to do that, my struggle ends in failure and defeat. I need You to take over my life and live Your life through me. I believe that You died on the cross for my sins, and You rose from the dead to bring me new life. I am sorry for all my sins. Please forgive me. I forgive anyone who has ever offended me. I open the door of my life and receive You as my Savior and Lord. I turn over my whole life, every detail of my life to You. Take control of my life. Help me to be the kind of person You want me to be. Thank You for forgiving my sins and giving me eternal life. Please send Your Holy Spirit upon me to fill me with love for the Father and for You and to guide and direct me in everything I do and say. Warn me of all impending danger to body or soul. Send Your angels to protect me of all harm. Lead me not into temptation, but deliver me from all evil. I ask this in Your name, Jesus Christ my Lord. Amen.

LEARNING HOW TO "BE STILL"

God, in all methods of prayer, must teach us how to be still. Mother Teresa of Calcutta offers these insights.

"If we really want to pray, we must first learn to listen, for in the silence of the heart, God speaks. And to be able to see that silence, to be able to hear God, we need a clean heart, for a clean heart can see God, can hear God, can listen to God.

When it is difficult to pray, we must help ourselves to do so. The first means to use is silence, for souls of prayer are souls of great silence. We cannot put ourselves directly in the presence of God if we do not practice internal and external silence.

God is the friend of silence.

Let us adore Jesus in our hearts, who spent thirty years out of thirty-three in silence, who began his public life by spending forty days in silence, who often retired alone to spend the night on a mountain in silence. He who spoke with authority, now spends his earthly life in silence. Let us adore Jesus in the eucharistic silence.

We need to find God and He cannot be found in noise and restlessness. See how nature, the trees, the flowers, the grass grow in perfect silence – see the stars, the moon and the sun, how they move in silence. Is not our mission to give God to the poor in the slums? Not a dead God but a living, loving God. The more we receive in silent prayer, the more we can give in our active life.

Silence gives us a new outlook on everything. We need silence to be able to touch souls. The essential thing is not what we say but what God says to us and through us. Jesus is always waiting for us in silence. In that silence He will listen to us, there He will speak to our soul, and there we will hear His voice. Interior silence is very difficult, but we must make the effort. In silence, we will find new energy and true unity. The energy of God will be ours to do all things well. The unity of our thoughts with His thoughts, the unity of our prayers with His prayers, the unity of our actions with His actions, of our life with His life. All our words will be useless, unless they come from within – words which do not give the light of Christ increase the darkness."

Deep prayer and contemplation are in response to the love of God. It does not start with active efforts or anxious striving on our part, but with love powerfully experienced. St. John is quite clear on this point; "In this is love, not that we loved God, but that He loved us." In the silence of our hearts, this love is like a call which is invariably creative – evoking a response, an interior movement of the soul toward God, energy. This is the energy which enables Mother Teresa and others like her to fuse a life of prayer with a life of action. The one is totally dependent on the other. Her tremendous achievements depend for their efficacy on a receptive, listening silence.

> *Lord,*
> *Teach us that even as the wonder of the stars in heaven only reveals itself in the silence of the night, so the wonder of God reveals itself in the silence of the soul. That in the silence of our hearts we may see the scattered leaves of all the universe bound by love.*
>
> *-- Adapted from the Bhagavad Gita*

STEPS TO BECOMING STILL
"Be still and know that I am God" (Ps 46:10)

What a beautiful image of prayer is found in that magnificent story of Elijah who heard God not in the thunder but in the still voice of the breeze.

We live on two consciousness levels. On the surface, at the level of the ego and marketplace, all sorts of hurried, frantic and distracting thoughts compete for attention. But deep within the Spirit of God is prayer. If we can learn to "go beneath" the outer self and center down, we could literally flow with the Spirit.

In order to become still, there are certain things that we can do.

Remove outer noise:
1. Remove outer noise. Get away from television, the telephone and other business around us. Go off by yourself to a quiet place.
2. Remove all physical tension by sitting in a comfortable location.
3. Tap into the quietness of the world in the early morning, or in the early or late evening.

Remove inner noise:
1. Still thoughts of things to do by writing them down so you will not forget them.
2. Still thoughts of sin. Confess your sin to Jesus and receive His forgiveness.

Resolve to go to confession if need be. Be bathed in the Blood of His forgiveness.

3. Still fluttering thoughts by focusing on Jesus. Say His name "Jesus" over and again, keeping time with your breathing.

4. Try to get in touch with your heart. Begin singing softly and listening to the spontaneous song bubbling up from your heart.

5. Driving the car or waiting at a red light is a wonderful time for quiet prayer. Some thoughts will begin to bubble forth, such as "My beloved child, listen carefully; all is well. Look only to Me. Listen to Me. I will guide you gently and for always. Stop. Look. Listen. Stop your frantic activity. Look unto Me. Listen to My words."

Write these down in a spontaneous flow to be discerned (sorted out) at a later time with Scripture, a spiritual director or friend in the Lord.

You will soon be able to sense inner stillness as:

1. Not doing anything. There is no striving or efforting, just relaxing and surrendering; in other words, letting go.

2. Being in touch with the Lord.

3. Experiencing His presence in the NOW, in the moment, knowing Him as the great "I AM."

4. Sharing this moment with His in love, praise and worship using your "inner eyes."

5. Something that is not forced or hurried.

6. Just allowing it to happen.

7. Experiencing an attitude of relaxed living.

8. Simply abiding, as a branch to a vine.

Examples of virtues required are:

Humility - Being willing to be alone with the Alone, being a child with his "Abba".

Contrition – Repenting of any known sin.

Fruit – Really believing that God is within us and wants to make His presence felt.

Patience – Giving Him all the time He wants.

Trust – Trusting Him to respond.

Discernment: How do I know if this is of God?

In these apocalyptic times, the question arises over and again, "How can I tell if something is coming from the Spirit of God?"

First of all, there are certain realities against which all discernment is placed:

- That God, our Father, has a wonderful plan that He reveals step-by-step and moment-by-moment both individually and collectively to His people.

- That this loving Father is covenanted to watch over, guide, nurture and protect His people.

- That this loving, covenanted plan is realized most fully in the person of Jesus, His Son, whom the Father sent as the Way, the Truth, and the Life.

- That Jesus has left His Spirit to guide His Body, the Church, down through the ages.

- That the Spirit speaks externally through the Church, the Bible, signs, sacraments, apparitions, events, people, symbols, experiences, and so forth; and He speaks internally through our thoughts, our deepest feelings, through dreams, visions and intuitions to each member of the Church personally and to the Church as a whole.

- That the final certainty of individual apparitions, dreams, and so forth lies with the whole Church, whom the Spirit protects from substantial error.

Therefore, in discernment, there are certain principles for individual discernment:

1. When I seek God with all my heart, I will find Him (cf Jer 31:34). When one is ready to die to self and seek only God, nine-tenths of the problems are overcome.

2. I seek the will of God as revealed by the Church and by the Spirit. The Inspiration, the teachings of the Church, and the Scriptures must be in line. What is of God will always be consistent with the Church and the Scriptures.

3. Next, take into account providential circumstances that will often point in one direction.

4. I seek wise counsel from a Spiritual Director or wise friend in the Lord.

5. Be willing to fast.

6. Look for the fruit. "By their fruits you shall know them."

7. Expect harassments and difficulties for Satan will not stand by idle.

8. Expect deep inner peace and joy despite the struggle.

9. Be willing to wait for doors to open.

> *When the idea / event is not of God,*
> *God says NO.*
>
> *When you are not right,*
> *God says GROW.*
>
> *When the time is not right,*
> *God says SLOW.*
>
> *When everything is right,*
> *God says GO!*

"If you really want to know what God wants you to do, simply ask Him. Make sure you really expect a solid answer for a double-minded person will be unsettled as a wave in the sea." (James 1:5-6)

SERENITY PRAYER

GOD GRANT ME THE SERENITY TO ACCEPT THE THINGS I CANNOT CHANGE, COURAGE TO CHANGE THE THINGS I CAN AND WISDOM TO KNOW THE DIFFERENCE.

PRINCIPLES OF DISCERNMENT

1. **"Trust in the Lord and He will bring you into the promised land"** (Ps. 37).

We must remember that God wants us to follow Him, and wants this for us far more than we want it. It is His responsibility to lead. Jeremiah 31:33 says, "I will place My law within them. I will be their God." So, start at the very beginning with God.

We must learn to trust in the Lord. In the book of the Prophet Isaiah, the Lord speaks to His people this way. "Thus says the Lord, your Redeemer, the Holy One of Israel: I, the Lord your God, teach you what is good for you. I lead you in the way that you must go." As we come to know the Lord, we come to understand that He wants to be our Shepherd, to lead us. Jesus came as our Advocate, our Counselor, and He sent His Holy Spirit to continue His mission.

The Lord wants us to know His direction for our lives. We can depend on it. The more we put our trust in the Lord and expect Him to lead us, the more we will be able to see the way. Faith in God's guidance is something that we can grow in just as we can grow in faith in other areas of our lives. As we grow in the Christian life, as we grow in the knowledge of the Lord, we grow in our faith that He will guide us. We need to put away all of our anxieties. We need simply to expect the Lord to make clearer to us what our life should become.

At first, we may be uncertain and often confused. We will never come to a time when we can know everything we want to know, but we can reach the point in our relationship with the Lord where we know that we can trust Him to guide us.

Enlighten the Darkness of My Heart

O Most High, Glorious God,
   enlighten the darkness of my heart and give me
   a right faith,
   a certain hope
   and a perfect love, understanding and knowledge,
O Lord,
   that I may carry out your holy and true command.
Amen.

-- Francis of Assisi

2. **"Delight in the Lord and He will give you the deepest desires of your own heart"** (Ps. 37).

The Will of the Father is not only demonstrated by external forces. In fact, it is primarily felt as an internal invitation. That which is the deepest, richest, holiest, truest, purest, most-loving reality within my spirit is the true God within me. Although this may be covered over by attitudes of my false ego, I can trust my deepest convictions.

As proof of this, ask yourself or your friends this question: "If you were really free, would you choose to be always loving, sometimes hateful and sometimes loving, or always hateful?" Very few of us would fail to choose the first alternative. You can substitute any of the fruits of the Spirit, such as joy, and the results would be the same. Deep down we all want to be all that which God wants us to be. The Kingdom of Heaven is within each of us. As we praise, honor, and delight in the Lord, He comes alive in us. This truth has to be practiced to be appreciated. The Lord inhabits the praise of His people.

As we delight in God, the deepest desires of our hearts become inflamed. The Holy Spirit speaks to our spirits. The beautiful thing about God is that He wants our best which is His best. He wants us to live in the Kingdom of love, joy, peace, patience, gentleness, faithfulness, and self-control. The gentle, revealing therapy of the Holy Spirit cuts away all dross in us so that the pure gold may shine forth. As I seek His Kingdom first, I find the Kingdom and all other good things that are inside of it.

3. **Commit your ways unto the Lord and He will make your holiness shine as the noonday sun** (Ps. 37).

In order to have God be God in my life, I must submit everything to Him: my intellect, my will, my emotions, my sexuality, my property, my money, my credit cards, my home, my family, my loved ones – everything. For God is totally responsible only for a life totally submitted to Him. God is the source and the reality.

Often it is "through the glass, darkly," that we are able to see. Therefore, it's not uncommon for us to see the psychiatrist, the physician, the banker, the scientist, the teacher, parent, husband, wife, friends, or ourselves as the source. However, this is an illusion. The Holy Spirit has to refocus our myopia and clear our vision until we can get our eyes fixed on Jesus, who is the "author and the finisher of my faith." (Heb. 12:4)

"In whom dwells all richness of the universe." He is my treasure, my romance, and my God. He is my shepherd, my physician, my priest, my deliverer, my all. I can commit everything into His loving care and relax and He will refine, purify, and strengthen my mind, my will, and my heart. "For the God of peace will make you perfect in Holiness and He will preserve you, whole and entire – spirit, soul and body unreproachable at the coming of Our Lord, Jesus Christ. He who calls us is trustworthy; therefore, He will do it" (Thes. 5:23-24).

Each of us needs to make a regular practice of offering our lives to the Lord. If we love the Lord, we want Him to rule our lives. Many people make this offering each morning; many people do it each time they pray or each time they participate in the Eucharist or other forms of worship.

Offering our lives to the Lord has to be more than just words. Behind those words each time we say them, there needs to be a commitment of our hearts to Him. Our offering does not make much difference unless we actually surrender our lives to Him. However, this should not make us undervalue the act of telling the Lord that we are making this offering. We are human beings; when we express our love, it grows. When we do not express it, it begins to fade. The more we express our desire to offer our lives to the Lord, the more the desire deepens in us, and the more deeply we orient our lives in the Lord's direction.

4. Obey what God has already told you.

God leads us step by step. He will not tell us the next thing to do until we have done the last thing. Psalm 6:28 says, "If I regard iniquity in my heart, the Lord will not hear me." The person who is obedient to God allows God to lead him into more and more of His special blessings and understands more about God and His will for his life. If there is known sin in your life, therefore, confess it, and resolve never to commit it again. You cannot have hatred in your heart and follow the God of Love; you cannot harbor resentment in your heart and follow the God of Compassion; you cannot nurture unforgiveness in your heart and follow the God of Forgiveness. You cannot have lust in your heart and follow the God of purity. Sin obscures the heart from seeing and/or doing the Will of God.

The primary prerequisite for knowing God's will, whether in general or in a specific issue, is obedience to His already-revealed Will. Many times, when a person is indecisive, confused, frustrated, or facing some misfortune, he needs to see where he may be in opposition to the Will of God. Obedience includes, not only following the issues at stake but, every aspect of our lives.

If God has already told you what action to take about a matter, you do not need to seek the counsel of others. You do not need to study or become involved with great religious acts, or even prayer. You do need to be obedient to what He has already revealed. Sometimes, we really do not want guidance. Instead, we want to alter the Will of God. We sometimes do not really want to know God's Will, but we want His sanction for our will. If we persist in this, we will inevitably end up like the children of Israel who lusted in the wilderness. God gave them their request but sent leanness into their souls.

5. Bring your heart into a state of poised indifference.

St. Paul states, "I have been initiated into a secret. I have learned to be content in any and all circumstances, on a full or empty stomach..." God gives us hot and cold, light and darkness, fullness and poverty, marriage and celibacy, good times and bad times, plenty and want. From this, we learn that God is the only important thing in our lives.

In our human weakness, we make material things and people the center of our lives; conferring on these things the status of God which then makes our center very weak. God knows that we need Him in the center, so he purifies us by bringing us into a state where we are able to let go of anything that He wishes us to.

A surrendered person is the one who prays with outstretched hands saying from the bottom of his/her heart, "Father take anything you want; leave anything you want. I want only You and Your Will for my life. If I am overly attached to any person or thing, take it from me or purify my heart in relationship to it. I am indifferent."

Often, our fear of what God may ask is greater than what God actually does ask. We must be willing to surrender all (including this fear), to learn that God usually takes only the things that are obstacles to our living His life to the full. He purifies much of what He takes, returns it to us, and we have more than before.

> Give God the bad,
>   and He will make it good!
> Give God the good,
>   and He will make it better!
> Give God the better,
>   and He will make it best!

We can see this in operation in Abraham's willingness to place Isaac on the sacrificial altar; the rich young ruler was asked to place his possessions on that altar. The disciples were asked to give up their families and professions. We, too, must be willing to give up everything for Christ, if this is His will. That beautiful Stations of the Cross prayer, "I love you, Jesus, my Love. I am sorry for ever having offended Thee. Grant that I may love Thee always and then do with me what You will," is a true and dangerous prayer. Expect God to answer it.

6. Be willing to fast.

The Lord tells us in Scripture that "As high as the heavens are above the earth, so high are My ways above your ways and My thoughts above your thoughts" (Is. 55:9). One way to get inside the mind of God in order to cooperate in His plan is, according to Scripture, by prayer and fasting. Fasting could be recommended for a number of reasons: it is good for your health, especially if you are overweight, and it is also good for the clearing of your mind.

Fasting is clearly associated with turning to the Lord, expressing our need for Him. In the Book of Jonah, after Jonah has preached God's word of repentance to the Ninevites, the King of Nineveh issued a decree, "Neither man nor beast, neither cattle, nor sheep shall taste anything; they shall not eat, nor shall they drink water. Man and beast shall be covered with sackcloth and call loudly to God, every man shall turn from his evil way and from the violence he has in hand."

Whether it is turning to the Lord in the sense of turning away from sin or a simple turning to Him in time of need, fasting accompanies prayer as a symbol of total dependence on God. When God breaks into our lives with the power of His Word, we want to leave everything; that is why it is most appropriate to lay aside eating and drinking for periods of time.

In Scripture, fasting is closely related to the Word of God. In Exodus, we are told that Moses went to Mt. Sinai and fasted for forty days and forty nights. It was during this fast that God revealed His Covenant to the Israelites. The prophet Elijah had been fasting for an extended period and God spoke to him in the tiny whispering sound (Kings 10). When we are in a position of total need before God, fasting before the Lord, His voice can come to us with power. Fasting is one of the ways we can open ourselves to God's gifts. We set aside a little of our own power, a little of our own desire for food and drink in order to depend more fully on God and allow His Spirit to nourish us.

Jesus illustrated this principle dramatically when, during a forty-day fast in the desert, He was tempted by Satan to turn stones into bread and He replied, "Not on bread alone is man to live but on every utterance that comes from the Mouth of God."

Fasting can put us in touch with the power of God by putting us in touch with the power of His Word. We find this also to be true in Daniel 10:2-3. Daniel fasted for Wisdom. And then, in Acts 13:2-2, where the Elders at Antioch were fasting and praying when the Lord spoke to them in prophecy: "Set apart Barnabas and Saul for Me to do the work for which I have called them; then after they had fasted and prayed they imposed hands on them and sent them off." This was the beginning of the mission to the Gentiles.

7. **Read the word of God daily and listen attentively to it whenever you hear it preached.**

God's Word, next to His Church, is the greatest created gift of God's Will. In Peter, 2:2-3, we read: "Like newborn babes, long for the pure milk of the Word that by it you may grow in respect to salvation if you have tasted the kindness of the Lord." Much of what God is going to say to us has already been said in His Word. Because God is the author of the Bible, the Bible is the greatest book that has ever been written.

God Himself speaks through the Bible to men and women of every age. It is "The Book par excellence," of Divine instruction. It offers comfort in sorrow, guidance in perplexity, advice for our problems, rebuke for our sins, and daily inspiration for our every need. By reading the Bible, we discover and are convicted of our sins. In reading the Bible, God imparts His strength to us and instructs us in what we are to do. The Bible provides us with the sword of victory over sin and makes our lives fruitful, and it gives us the power to pray.

The Bible, however, is not an end in itself, but it is a means to the end of knowing God and doing His Will. The apostle Paul said, "Be diligent to present yourselves approved to God as a workman who does not need to be ashamed handling accurately the Word of Truth. (2 Tim. 2:15)

PRACTICAL SUGGESTIONS FOR BIBLE READING

A. **Begin your Bible reading with a prayer.** (Ps. 118:18, Jn. 16:13-15)

B. **Take brief notes on what you read.** Keep a small notebook handy for your Bible study.

C. **Read slowly through one chapter or perhaps two or three, even one paragraph or verse at a time.** After reading, ask yourself the following questions and then write the answers in your notebook. Not all questions may be answered each time.

   a. What is the main subject of the passage?
   b. Who are the persons revealed in the passage? Who is speaking? About whom is he speaking? Who is acting, etc.?
   c. What is the key verse of the passage?
   d. What does the passage teach me about the Lord Jesus?
   e. Is there any sin for me to confess and forsake in the passage?
   f. Is there any command for me to obey in the passage?
   g. Is there any promise for me to claim?
   h. Is there any instruction for me to follow?
   i. Is there any prayer that I should pray?

D. **Keep a spiritual diary** either in your Bible study notebook or in a separate notebook entitled "My Spiritual Diary." Write down daily what God says to you through the Bible. Write down the sins that you confess or the commands you should obey.

E. **Memorize passages of God's Word.** No one is ever too old to memorize the Word of God. Write key verses on cards with references to one side and the verse on the other. Carry these cards in your pocket and review them while waiting for a bus, plane, standing in line, etc.

F. **Obey the Word of God.** As Paul said to Timothy in 2 Tim. 3:16, "All Scripture is inspired by God and profitable for teaching, for reproof, for correction, for training in righteousness."

Do not adopt all of these methods at once, but start out slowly, selecting those methods and suggestions which appeal to you. You will find, as millions of others have done before you, that the more you read and study the Word of God, the more you will want to read it.

8. **Learn to apply God's Word.** Every verse in the Bible is profitable for us, but not every verse in the Bible is directly applicable to us. (Tim. 3:16-17)

First, we must learn what the major themes are in the Bible, which run throughout the Scriptures. Father Richard Rohr has developed insightful tapes discussing the major themes of Scripture. As we learn what these themes are, we can better understand the related doctrines and practices. The Pharisees lost sight of this and focused on the minutiae of the law. In the process, they forgot about the importance of loving God and loving their fellow man.

Frequently, cults will do this by taking an isolated verse and then building a whole doctrinal system. Heresy is taking any truth of the Bible and giving it more weight than corresponding truths, such as has been done with the Divinity-Humanity of Christ. Keeping this in balance has challenged the Church throughout the ages.

Second, remember to properly apply God's Word so as not to overextend or make an over-inclusive application of a verse or truth. The initial truth is correct but if applied too far, it goes beyond the scope of the intent of the Holy Spirit. Once again, overemphasized truth is a heresy.

Third, understand that some verses are not applicable in some situations. They were only intended for a specific situation. For example, when Paul addressed the problem of women, sitting out of hearing range, calling out loud to find out what was being said, by saying women should not speak in Church, Paul was not saying that all women were to be quiet always in Church; only not to call out when they could not hear.

Fourth, realize that much of the Bible contains examples to teach us principles rather than specific literal commands that one must follow if he/she is to please God. I think it is obvious that we are not required to obey ordinances such as the sacrificial offerings of animals commanded in the Old Testament. Bill Gothard is very good in his own bringing forth Biblical principles.

Fifth, be sure that the qualifications for application are both met and realized. For instance, Isaiah 55:11 indicates that "God's Word shall not return unto Me void." When we were babes in the Scriptural life, God wanted us to learn how to pray in Christ's name. But, as we grow, He expects us to learn and apply more of the qualifications for prayer. He expects us to use both "the whole council of God" (Acts 20:27).

Sixth, be sure to avoid self-serving use of the Bible. The Word of God is as much misused as it is used. Some people misuse Scripture because they read into it their own biases, prejudices, and traditions.

Seventh, ask and listen to the Spirit. We read in James 1:5-8, "If you really want to know what God wants you to do, ask Him and He will gladly tell you; for He is always ready to give a bountiful supply of Wisdom to all who ask Him. He will not resent your asking, but when you ask Him, be sure that you really expect Him to tell you, for a doubtful mind will be as unsettled as the wave of the sea that is driven and tossed by the wind." And, every decision you then make will be uncertain as you turn first this way and then that.

If you do not ask with faith, do not expect the Lord to give you any solid answer. For Jesus says, "Ask and you will receive. Seek and you will find. Knock and it shall be opened unto you." Jesus also said, "How much more will My Father give the Holy Spirit to those who ask Him." Ask God everything. Take nothing for granted.

Eighth, the person who desires to know God's Will must have a life of prayer. The Scriptures clearly teach that a consistent prayer life is mandatory. Daniel prayed faithfully three times a day, and the Psalmists prayed probably seven times a day. It is recorded that Christ rose early in the morning to pray and at times spent hours in prayer. And Paul spoke of "praying without ceasing" (1 Thes: 5:17).

An integral part of a life of prayer is not so much asking or even talking to God, but listening and meditating. Much of God's will is learned precisely in this way. Isaiah 41 says, "Listen to Me in silence." "Let them approach, then let them speak." The Psalmist say, "The meditation of my heart shall be understanding." (Ps. 49:3)

Prayer is a conversation between myself and God, in which God does most of the talking. If I were having a conversation with a brilliant doctor, hopefully, I would let him do most of the talking. If I were talking to the greatest scientist in the world, once again, I would allow him to do most of the talking. The same is true in prayer. I should do most of the listening and God should do most of the talking.

In addition to a life of prayer and meditation, the Bible teaches us to pray specifically when we want to know His Will about a particular matter. The gift of wisdom is the tool that God provides to help us make the right decisions. It is the gift that enables us to discover God's plan and to move with it and to keep on moving with it. Wisdom is that gift that enables us not to get ahead of the Lord, not get far behind Him, but be His side. The gift of Wisdom can tell you what you need to do in every circumstance.

9. Wait upon the Spirit.

Jesus says "He charged them to wait for the promise of the Father which He said you heard from me" (Acts 1:4). In the life of all the Old Testament saints, waiting was one of the love words in which they expressed the posture of their soul towards God. They waited for God and waited upon God. Sometimes, we find it is Holy Scripture as a language of an experience. "Truly my soul waited upon God. I wait for the Lord, my soul does wait." At other times, there is a plea and prayer, "Lead me. On you I do wait all the day." Frequently, it is an injunction encouraging us to persevere in work that is not without its difficulties, "Wait on the Lord. Wait I say on the Lord. Rest in the Lord and wait patiently for Him."

The Holy Spirit is not given to us as a possession of which we have charge in mastering, in which we can use at our discretion. The Holy Spirit is given to us to be our Master and have charge of us. It is not we who are to use Him. He is indeed ours, but ours as God, and our position toward Him is that of deep and entire dependence on one who gives to everyone even as He will. The Father has indeed given us the Spirit who only works as the Spirit of the Father. Our asking for His working that the Father would grant unto us to be strengthened with might by His Spirit, and our waiting for this, must be as real and definite as if we had to ask for Him for the first time.

When God gives us His Spirit, He gives us His inmost self. He gives with

Divine giving that is in the power of eternal life, that which is continuous, uninterrupted, and never-ceasing. When Jesus gave His believers the promise of a fountain of ever-flowing streams; He spoke, not of a single act of faith which was a once-for-all to make them independent possessors of that blessing; but a life of faith, faith that its never-ceasing receptivity would always and only possess His gift in loving union with Himself – and so this precious word – wait.

10. Be open to the Holy Spirit.

To know God's Will, we must not only acknowledge the person of the Holy Spirit but also allow Him to control our lives. Christ tells us that the Spirit is given to every believer. However, we are further told, in fact commanded, that we should be filled with the Holy Spirit. God wants to fill us with the Holy Spirit as we allow Him to control more areas of our lives. We can have as much of Him as we really want.

God has revealed Himself in two great dispensations. In the Old Testament, we have the time and promise in preparation. In the New Testament, we have fulfillment and possession. In harmony with the difference of the two dispensations, there is a two-fold working of God's Holy Spirit.

Before Christ, in the Old Testament, we have the Spirit of God coming upon men and working on them in special times and ways – God worked from above and without working inwards. In the New Testament, after Christ, we have the Holy Spirit entering and living within man, then working from within – outwards and upwards. In the former, God is the Almighty, the Holy One; in the latter, we have the Spirit of the Father of Jesus Christ.

The difference between the two-fold operation of the Holy Spirit is not to be regarded as if – with the closing of the Old Testament – the former ceased, and there was – in the New – no more other work of preparation. By no means is this true. Just as in the Old Testament, there was blessed anticipation of the indwelling of God's Spirit, so now, in the New Testament, the two-fold working still continues.

According to the language or knowledge of faith, a believer may get little beyond the first half of the promise. The spirit's initial work in convicting of sin and of holiness is His leading to repentance and faith; and the new life, is but a preparatory work. The distinctive glory of the dispensation of the Spirit is His Divine personal indwelling in the heart of the believer, there to reveal the Father and His Will for our lives. It is only as Christians understand and remember this, that they will be able to claim the full blessing prepared for them in Christ Jesus.

In the words of Ezekiel, we find in one promise this two-fold blessing (which God bestows through His Spirit) very strikingly set forth. The first is "I will put within you a new Spirit." That is man's own spirit is to be renewed and quickened by the work of God's Spirit. When this has been done, there is a second blessing: "I will put My Spirit within you to dwell in the new spirit. Where God is to dwell, He must have a habitation."

11. Be open to the natural.

Sometimes He leads us through supernatural, miraculous methods discussed earlier. This may mean a voice, a vision, or a dream; however, the far-more common way He leads is in a deep inward assurance that a given thing is God's will. This is exemplified in Luke 2:27, which says, "The Holy Spirit had impelled Him to go." There is a deep sense of rightness that we should do a certain thing and that it is in no way contrary to God's Will. This assurance is accompanied by a deep sense of peace.

Exodus 33:14 says, "My presence will go with you and I will give you rest." The Holy Spirit's leading is always consistent with scripture and authentic tradition, and with enlightened reason and judgment. From the external perspective, it makes sense.

12. Talk things over with those who are wiser in the Lord; get counsel.

Our primary counsel regarding God's Will should come from God Himself through the Word of God and also, directly. However, there are times when God uses the counsel of others to help us know His Will. A spiritual guide is not so much one who directs us but one who helps us discern what the Lord is saying to us. This guide is one who walks by our side, not one who stands between us and God.

The writer of Proverbs knew the value of good counselors when he wrote, "where no counsel is, the people fail, but in the multitude of counselors, there is safety" (Prov. 15:22). Without counsel, plans go wrong, but with many advisors, they succeed. "He that harkens unto counsel is wise. Get all the advice you can and be wise the rest of your lives."

The aim of counsel should be clearly understood. In some instances, it is primarily to give information. A student seeks advice from a school counselor regarding classes and requirements for certain courses. We go to a physician to diagnose and remedy a health problem. When seeking spiritual counsel, we sometimes find that we may have a blind spot in a particular area that we overlook and it is only through the aid of a gentle, spiritual, counselor that we eventually see.

At other times, we seek counsel to help us clarify our thoughts, and see truth. Even if we hear the Lord speaking to us in a personal way, it is sometimes difficult for us to see clearly and possess the sureness we need without talking things over with a trusted advisor. The Lord wants us to be members of His body, receiving guidance from Him and from the other members of the body. As we talk with others about our concerns, we become more sure of our sense of direction. There is a temptation to live too much inside ourselves, to seek direction only on our own. We must always be aware that Satan lives in the dark and works in secret.

Conversely, the Lord is light and truth. In the Gospel of John, we read, "Anyone who does evil things hates the light and will not come to the light because he does not want his evil deed to be shown up. But, whoever does what is true comes to the light in order that the light may show that He did his works in obedience to God." The more we live in the light, out in the open, allowing other Christians to see us, the safer we will be.

Talking things over with others can and should mean talking things over with people who are older and wiser in the Lord, or those who are in authority over us in the Lord. Each of us should seek pastoral or spiritual direction from our pastors or retreat houses with some regularity. It also means discussing our lives and our plans with other Christians. We should learn to share our lives in a personal way and to discuss what is happening with us in a personal way. As we do, we will see the Lord begin to give us guidance in our daily conversation with other Christians.

A word of caution regarding counseling. We should never seek or listen to counsel from people if "The Counselor, God" has already spoken on the subject. There are times when God may specifically direct us not to seek counsel. Paul, you will remember, went into the desert and specifically avoided the counsel of Christ's disciples.

On the other hand, seeking counsel from others is God's appointed means of revealing His Will. Proverbs 10:8 says, "The wise man is glad to be instructed, but a self-sufficient fool falls flat on his face." Pride keeps many people from seeking help from others and may ultimately prevent them from knowing God's Will. It is important to seek counsel from the right individuals. Some people run from one person to another seeking advice. Chances are they just want to talk about their problems and indecision, and really are not seeking counsel at all. Others seek advice only from those who will condone what they have already decided to do.

Be careful of wrong counsel. Psalm 1:1 warns us about obtaining counsel from the wicked. However, even well-meaning friends, at times, may give us the wrong advice. The counsel of Job's friends, you will recall, was unsolicited and very ill-advised. The ten spies gave wrong counsel to the children of Israel and it cost them 40 more years in the dry, parched desert. Paul warns us that though we start out well, the wrong persuasion can adversely affect our entire life. Sometimes, even Christian leaders are capable of giving us wrong counsel. Peter was wrong when he compelled the Gentiles to live like Jews. We are warned that even if leaders claim they have seen a vision and specific directions in which you are to go, they may still be wrong. We are advised to refuse such counsel.

13. Do not seek a ministry, but the fruits of a disciplined life.

So often we fail to recognize that God is primarily interested in making us sons and daughters. He is more interested in doing this than in making us priests, evangelists, or prophets. God wants us to be totally surrendered to Him as His children. Many people want a tremendous evangelistic ministry; and yet, God is simply asking them to take the first step in loving Him in a child-like way. For example, more than a healing ministry, Catherine Kulman had a listening ministry. The Lord would simply whisper to her "over here, I'm healing someone; Catherine, over here, now." She would simply listen and then call it forth.

14. In all your ways, make Christ known and He will direct your path.

If we really preach about Christ, sometimes that will cause us so much of a problem that it will lead us out of a wrong job and into the right one. If we really seek first the Kingdom of God, God is free to allow the circumstances of our lives either to come against us and move us on; or as it happened so often in the early Church, to move us into something that He wants us to share with Him.

15. Look for providential circumstances.

It's amazing all the things that "just happen" throughout the Old Testament and the New Testament. For example, we see God's guidance in Joseph's life. His brothers wanted to kill him but decided to throw him into a deep hole in the ground that "just happened" to be nearby. Then, a caravan to Egypt "just happened" by and Joseph was sold to the traders. A certain job, a satisfied employer, a vengeful woman, prison, the right acquaintances, dreams, and famine, plus much more were all further means which God used to lead Joseph to his position of Second-in-Command of all Egypt.

It's interesting to consider if Joseph had any idea that the circumstances of his life were part of God's Providential guidance. However, years later in retrospect, he could say to his brothers, "God did it. He sent me there ahead of you to preserve your lives. God turned into good what you meant for evil. For He brought me to this fine position I have today so that I could save the lives of many people" (Gen. 45:5; 50:20).

In the incidence of Saul being led to his anointing in Joseph's pilgrimage, the providential circumstances led them without much initiative or evaluation required on their part. They were more or less forced into situations. However, providential circumstances often open doors of opportunity that we must evaluate and for which we then must take appropriate action if God's desired results are to be achieved. Esther exemplifies this, as does Paul's finding doors opened for him to preach the Gospel. However, it's important to note that circumstances themselves do not constitute Divine guidance.

16. The Magisterium of the Church

Note the "signs of the times" seen in this very beautiful letter that Pope John Paul II gave to the French Bishops on June 1, 1980:

> "The mission of the Church, which is continually realized in the eschatological perspective is, at the same time, fully historical. That is connected with the duty of reading 'the signs of the times', which was so deeply considered by Vatican-II. With great perspicacity, the Counsel also defined what the mission of the Church is in the present state of history.

> Our common task remains, therefore, the acceptance and implementation of Vatican II, according to its authentic content. Doing so, we are guided by faith: it is our main and fundamental reason for acting. We believe that Christ, through the Holy Spirit, was with the councillar Fathers, and that the Council contains, in its magisterium, what the

Spirit 'says to the Church'; and that He says it at the same time in full harmony with tradition and according to the requirements dictated by the 'signs of the times.'

The faith is based on Christ's promise: 'I am with you always, to the close of the age' (Mt. 38:20). On this faith is founded also our conviction that we must 'implement the Council', such as it is, and not as some people would like to see and understand it.

There is nothing surprising about the fact that, in this 'postconciliar' stage, there have also developed, quiet intensely, certain interpretations of Vatican II, which do not correspond to its authentic magisterium. It is a question here of two well-known trends: 'progressivism' and 'integralism.'

The first are always eager to adapt even the content of faith, Christian ethics, the liturgy, ecclesial organization, to changes of mentalities, and to the demands of the 'world,' without sufficiently taking into account not only the general feeling of the faithful, who are bewildered, but also the essentials of the faith, already defined, the roots of the Church, her centuries-old experience, the norms necessary for her faithfulness, her unity, her universality.

They are obsessed about 'advancing' but toward what 'progress' when all is said and done?

The others – pointing out these abuses which we are, of course, the first to condemn and correct – adopt an intransigent attitude, shutting themselves up in a given period of the Church, at a given stage of theological formulation of liturgical expression which they make an absolute, without sufficiently penetrating its underlying meaning, without considering the totality of history and its legitimate development, fearing new questions, without admitting, in a word, that the Spirit of God is at work in the Church today, with her Pastors united with the Successor of Peter.

These facts are not surprising if we think of similar phenomena in the history of the Church. But, it is all the more necessary to concentrate all forces on correct, that is, authentic interpretation of the conciliar magisterium, as the indispensable foundation of the further self-realization of the church, for which this magisterium is the source of correct inspirations and orientations.

The two extreme trends which I have pointed out foster not only an opposition, but a regrettable and harmful division, as if they stirred up each other to the extent of creating uneasiness for everyone, even scandal, and of expending in this mutual suspicion and criticism so many energies which would be so useful for a real renewal."

There are actually three principles of discernment here. First, is what the reader thinks God is saying to him in accord with the authentic tradition of the Church? Second, is it in accord with the present teaching of the magisterium of the Church which will be based upon and in full harmony with tradition? Third, is it in accord with the requirements dictated by the signs of the times?

A discerning person, in other words, must be rooted in his tradition under the magisterium of the authentic leaders of the Church and implementing the present Gospel according to the signs of the times.

Authoritative teaching ... is seen as a hindrance to true liberty of conscience. To be truly adult, it is maintained, one's conscience must be formed exclusively from one's own insights, without reference to the authoritative teaching of the Church ...

However, it is precisely because conscience is so fallible in its insight into moral truth that such guidance has been provided by Christ. To expect to get along on one's own in moral matters, independently of all authority, is to run away from reality. It is a sign, not of maturity, but of immaturity ...

"The sense of right and wrong, which is the first element in religion, is so delicate, so fitful, so easily puzzled, obscured, perverted, so subtle in its argumentative methods, so impressionable by education, so biased by pride and passion, so unsteady in its course, that, in the struggle for existence amid the various exercises and triumphs of the human intellect, this sense is at once the highest of all teachers, yet the least luminous; and the Church, the Pope, the Hierarchy are, in the Divine purpose the supply of an urgent demand." (cf. Letter to the Duke of Norfolk) ...

Should the case arise, Pope John Paul II says, where one feels unable in conscience to obey a directive of the Pope, obedience to one's conscience certainly comes first ... But the decision to go against the Pope's authority can only be taken for the gravest of reasons:

"Unless a man is able to say to himself as in the presence of God, that he must not, and dare not, act upon the papal injunction, he is bound to obey it, and would commit a great sin by disobeying it" ...

17. **Have I submitted my decision to the elders that are placed over me for their discernment in the situation.**

Am I a submitted person? Do I stand under someone? Am I under some authority? This has placed certain leaders in the Church and they are the ones who will lead their people. We read in Ephesians, "God has given some to be apostles, some to be prophets, some to be evangelists, and teachers for the job of equipping the saints for the work of the ministry in order to build up the Body of Christ."

We read in Colossians that the foundation of the Church, in addition to Jesus Christ, is also "the Apostles and Prophets" because it is they who stand under God. An apostle and prophet, by definition, are "into God." The apostle is the one who is the architect of the Church who has received his mission from God to be a builder of a New Testament community; and a prophet, by definition, is one who listens to the Lord.

18. **Am I submitted to the apostles, the prophets, the pastors, and the elders that God has placed over me?**

God is not calling forth "lone rangers." He is calling people who are rooted within the Church. So much harm could be avoided if we simply understood this fact. Beware of the lone prophet. Beware of the lone ranger.

19. **Evaluation**

We must be willing to evaluate what we feel the Spirit is saying to us. We must take all of these principles and use as many of them as possible. Careful evaluation requires that we first have all the necessary information available, and then be willing to consider the factors for and against a given decision and the source and importance of each factor. We must consider the effects of whatever decisions are made.

Careful evaluation must include all the major guideposts discussed earlier: an openness to any means of God's leading, including the miraculous, and awareness of what God's Word says on the subject; openness to the Spirit's leading, praying for His guidance; seeking counsel if needed, and consideration of the providential circumstances; and consideration of what the Church and tradition and the signs of the times are saying. However, His voice from all other sources must always agree. The Scriptures, the promptings of the Holy Spirit, any miraculous leading from God, and what the Church is presently teaching, must be in accord, or at least not contradicting one another since God never contradicts Himself.

The Scriptural basis for evaluation is woven throughout the Bible. Samuel told Saul, "At that time, the Spirit of the Lord will come mightily upon you. From that time on, your decisions should be based on whatever seems best under the circumstances, for the Lord will guide you." The writer of Hebrews admonishes that: "solid food is for full-grown men." For those whose senses and mental faculties are trained by practice to discriminate and distinguish what is morally good and noble, and what is evil and contract either to Divine or human law.

Philip's translation puts if this way: "The man who has developed, by experience, his power to discriminate between what is good and what is bad for him." Paul adds further, "The spiritual man judges all things."

Once we begin to evaluate, Satan will try to confuse the issues. One way he does this is to encourage us to rely upon our feelings. A feeling is a strong inner leading toward something. The basis of that feeling may be good or bad. For our feelings are the result of a lifetime of various internal and external stimuli. This may include mixed-up emotions, impure motives, prejudices, or old thought patterns. There are usually five sources of our thoughts or our impressions:

1. The Holy Spirit
2. Satan and evil spirits
3. Other people
4. Systems of this world
5. Our own unredeemed selves.

God's voice is always what is best; as the poem states;

It is not always open ill
That risks the promised rest
The better often is the foe
That keeps us from God's best

The Holy Spirit is the selector of the right path – many times, between two good things – one being of God and the other not His will at the present time.

There would be no problem if we always recognized the voice of the Father. However, He usually disguises Himself through people, pressures, etc. Therefore, most of the loud voices we hear are either from within our own desires and impressions, or from the people about us. In either case, these impressions may be of God or not. We may have legitimate desires and needs that should be considered. At the same time, we know that our hearts can be deceitful and sinful and we know that people may help us or they may try to manipulate us for their own selfish ends – even in spiritual things.

The pressure to please people is also a problem. Sometimes you want to gain their favor. And then there is the tremendous pressure to help keep the machinery of the Churches and their organizations running. This, too, may be a good or a bad thing.

Even if the matter you are considering is good, scriptural, and desperately needed, it does not necessarily mean that God is calling you to pursue that course of action, at least not at this time. God is telling each one of us to do a specific thing at a specific time in a specific way. We have to be very discerning to find out what that is. We have to be willing to submit ourselves, our motives, our feelings in the matter.

Realize, however, that if we are yielded to Him, then God's will often comes through our own desires. Be careful about undertaking evaluation on any important decision when you are tired. Your thought processes and decisions can be adversely affected by fatigue. God had Elijah get plenty of sleep and adequate nourishment before He revealed His will further to him.

Whenever possible, avoid making on-the-spot decisions, even about small things. Get alone and give yourself plenty of time to prayerfully consider the matter. If someone is really pressuring you, that should raise your suspicion about the matter, although it may still be God's will for you.

One of the ways that may be helpful in making an evaluation is to take a piece of paper and list all of the pros and cons in a given situation. Then, try to discern what spirits are moving in between the pros and cons. Try to discern the motives behind things. Are there motives for lust, for gain? Are the real motives trying to help really discern what spirits are moving? Now, prayerfully, ask the Holy Spirit to help us select what He is saying through the various pros and cons. As we lay the matter before the Lord, we can usually discern the motives. As we consider alternatives, do not rush into a decision.

Meditate on the fact prayerfully asking God's will. Meditation can help clarify the sources of our feelings and help solidify a decision. When King Hesekiah received a distressing letter, he went up to the House of the Lord and spread it before the Lord. He prayed, allowing God to help clarify the issues and God answered his prayers (2 Kg. 11:14-21). Making important decisions alone with God without any pressure is crucial. Evaluation is the essential part of divine guidance where we bring together the various means of evidence, consider the weight of each, and allow the Holy Spirit to enlighten our understanding so that we make the right choice in determining God's will. Remember, the Holy Spirit is the selector of the best way.

20. Be willing to wait or to act.

Once you know God's will – you again need to bring yourself into poised indifference. Is now the acceptable time, or is He telling you to wait? We know that, at one point, Jesus knew the apostles were not ready so He told them to wait until the Holy Spirit was given to them. After having taken the previous steps in determining God's will in a matter, the time arrives to decide to wait or to decide to act. There must be an active choice. Not to decide is to decide. The decision to wait is a decision. It is an active decision. No choice is a choice. Indecision will lead to a choice by default, which is a poor choice.

If a person's heart is basically right before God and he prayerfully makes a choice that is wrong; that may, at times, be better than the choices made by a person who is constantly in the state of indecision. It is important to be moving. God can change the course but God really cannot get you up out of the boat and put you in the water unless you decide to take that first step out. One should never take the responsibility of knowing God's will and making the right decision lightly. However, God has occasionally intervened when the wrong decision was made by a person living in God's will. We, however, should not rely upon such intervention (2 Sam. 7:1-4).

Good decision making has several characteristics: It involves obtaining the necessary facts and evaluating them, as discussed earlier, when it involves the will of God, and it necessitates personal obedience. The evaluation and decision should be made alone – away from the pressures of time or people, if at all possible.

It is ideal and usually possible to prayerfully make the decision and then to wait on it; that is, decide what your course of action should be but delay implementing it for a while. The period of delay may vary from a few minutes, to hours, days, or occasionally, years. You may want to share the decision with a confidant, but it is best not to tell others about your decision immediately. If you do, it is a lot more difficult to alter that decision later.

This period of delay gives the Holy Spirit time to reaffirm the correctness of the decision or if it is out of God's will, He will cause you to be uneasy and allow the opportunity to change in the decision. One famous man of God said, "I have come to deliberate judgment according to the best of my ability and knowledge, and if my mind is thus at peace and continues so after two or three more petitions, I proceed accordingly."

Be slow to take new steps in the Lord's service or in your business or in your families. Weigh everything well. Isaiah 28:16 says, "He who believes will not be in haste." Proverbs 12:2 says, "It is dangerous and simple to rush into the unknown." That famous admonition, "fools rush in where angels fear to tread" is to be heeded. The stamp of approval is God's peace. "He will keep in perfect peace all those who trust in Him, whose thoughts turn often to the Lord. Oh Lord, we love to do your will. Our hearts desire to glorify your name" (Is. 26:3-8).

What a tremendous promise to obedient Christians. To the one living in God's Will, not merely peace, but perfect peace. He not only promises this perfect peace, but He also wants it to permeate our lives. The Scriptures speak of His peace as the umpire or arbitrator in our hearts. Colossians 3:15 puts it this way, "And let the peace from Christ rule." Let that peace act as a referee continually in your heart, deciding and settling with finality all questions that arise in your mind. (Amplified translation)

This does not mean that a person living in God's Will is free from problems or difficulties. It is in the same verse that assures us of this inward peace, that also reminds us that we will have trial, tribulations, and sorrows in the world. (John 16:33) There may be brief periods of time where there is turmoil, anguish, or agitation of Spirit. Peter was inwardly perplexed when God was leading him to a new area of service (Acts 10:17).

There may also be a time of struggle with the flesh, as our wills are aligned with His. During this time, what is God's Will is very clear through the major guideposts described earlier, and a deep sense of oughtness and peace from the Holy Spirit. As we yield our will to God, the oughtness will be accomplished by the growing peace of the Comforter (Acts 9:31).

When we are living in God's Will, the peace of God will rule as the loving Father, the observing umpire. When we prayerfully contemplate a course of action or a new step in our Christian life, God's peace will permeate our lives. This is one of the major functions of the Holy Spirit – to bring peace – a deep internal confidence that we are in His will.

The more our life points to God's perfect will (like a compass), the more His sanction of peace will rest upon us. There will be an inward joy and reassurance that we are walking in His life. After you have taken the steps described in the previous principles, you may be assured that if a pondered decision is in God's will, there will be an increased sense of rightness and peace. This is God's stamp of approval on that direction in your life – the umpire calls "safe."

"Now may the Lord of Peace Himself give you peace at all times, in all ways" (Thes. 3:16).

All of this can be summarized in two words, Yes and Abba. To say "Yes" to the Father in the moment is to be a saint at that moment and to live in the Kingdom of God at that moment. Mary's prayer was "Yes." And Jesus is the "Yes" to the Father. St. Paul tells us of all the many promises of God, Jesus is the "Yes" to them all. There's a simple poem which can be sung:

I say "Yes, Yes, Yes."
I say "Yes, Yes, Yes."
I say "Yes, My Lord."
I say "Yes, My Lord."
I say "Yes, Yes, Yes."

LISTENING TO THE FATHER

Fr. Bill McCarthy

Matthew 6:9-15 "Teach us to pray ... Our Father ... forgive ... ask, seek and knock..."

God has a plan for us individually and collectively.

God's plan was to send Jesus into the world and into our hearts, enabling us to think, love and act like Jesus and the Power to do that (the Holy Spirit) has been poured into us giving us the wisdom-gifts, the heart-gifts, and the power-gifts of the Holy Spirit.

Prayer – is a conversation where we talk to God and more importantly, God talks to us.

– is a two-way street, and the one with the greater message should have more time to speak, i.e., God.

Kinds of Prayer: Formal prayer, informal prayer, meditative prayer, prayer of anguish, prayer of faith - hope - love - contrition, contemplative power.

If we meet and you forget me,
you have lost nothing;
but if you meet JESUS CHRIST
and you forget Him you
have lost everything.

People of Prayer in Scripture

Moses - face reflected God's glory, Ex 34:33, 35

   - 2 Cor 3:13-16 - "But we, with unveiled faces, reflect like mirrors the brightness of the Son, who is our glory. For it is the work of the Spirit to change us from glory into glory into Him whom we reflect."

Mary - listened and did the will of the Father.
   - Annunciation - Lk 1:26-38

   The message of prayer: "Everyone is called to be the Mother of Jesus," i.e., to allow Jesus to be born within us. How? Through the Holy Spirit. Nothing is impossible for God "behold the handmaid of the Lord."

Jesus - John 5 - Jesus heals the man on the Sabbath
   The heart of the message of prayer is life more abundantly and life is a relationship with the Sourse of Life, the Father.

   The essence of Jesus' prayer is Jesus saying "Yes" to the still voice of the Father – doing only what the Father tells Him to do.

   Prayer is learning always to listen to God talking to us.

How Does God Talk To Us

Externally - through the Bible, the Church, experiences, signs, symbols, sacraments, nature, science, etc.

Internally - in new dispensation of God places His own Spirit within us, working from within, upward.

Thoughts - God's most often way of speaking to you is through your own thoughts.

   - the first six gifts of the Holy Spirit are thought-gifts: wisdom, understanding, knowledge, prophecy, conscience and discernment.

   - God put His own Spirit within you to enlighten your minds and inflame your hearts to know and to desire to do of His good pleasure.

> *"My God, I love Thee."*
> *(The best and shortest prayer)*

Desires - God speaks to you through your desires. If He wants you to do something, He will put the desire into your heart. Your deepest desire - to be what God wants you to be - was given to you by the Holy Spirit.

- God moves us through our insights and through the desires of the heart to know and to will His good pleasure. Heart gifts: love, compassion, sensitivity, caring, zeal, purity of heart, forgiveness.

Our Spirit - God speaks to us through our spirit, i.e., intuition.

Our Dreams - God speaks to us through our dreams.

HOW DO WE LISTEN TO GOD

Keep a Spiritual Journal

Step 1 - go off by yourself, become comfortable, close your eyes.

Step 2 - ask the Holy Spirit to quiet you down and when you are inwardly quiet, to give you a message.

Step 3 - think "Jesus" over and over again.

Step 4 - let daily preoccupations go by.

Step 5 - after you're quiet and absorbed in the Lord, because you have asked for it and because God wants to talk to you, a new message will come into your mind. Stop thinking the word and be aware of what things come to you. Begin writing. This, most likely, is God's message to you.

Step 6 - at some later date, be willing to show it to someone, or take it into some discernment process. After discernment, you must step out in faith and God will confirm it.

Praying with Scripture

The purpose is not just to get the words, but rather to find out what the Holy Spirit is saying to you through these words.

Step 1 - go to a quiet place

Step 2 - put yourself in the presence of God.

Step 3 - make it personal - what is God saying to you?

Step 4 - get the point that God has there for you - something that "jumps out at you" - stop reading.

Step 5 - after you get the point, and it's a personal point, discern it.

Step 6 - after you've discerned that what you're getting is from the Lord, then put it into action.

Prayer of Quiet

Contemplative prayer - just looking at God and God looking at you – heart to heart and much deeper than words.

The summary of prayer: YES. ABBA!

ROMANS 12:1-2   JAMES 1:5

A POWERFUL PRAYER TO BE SAID BEFORE PRAYING
"Almighty Father, I place the Precious Blood of Jesus before my lips before I pray, that my prayers may be purified before they ascend to Your divine altar."
-- *St. Mary Magdalen de Pazzi*

HABAKKUK - A BIBLICAL MODEL

My Experience of Inwardly Quieting Down and Allowing Jesus to Speak

1. I still myself in the Lord's presence most often through worship, singing in the Spirit or devotionally entering into a scripture passage. My outer being is quieted: my inner being is quieted. I am in neutral, poised before my Lord.

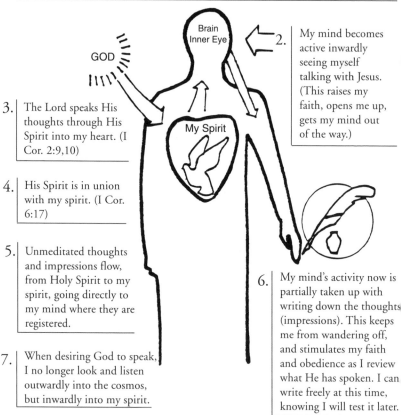

2. My mind becomes active inwardly seeing myself talking with Jesus. (This raises my faith, opens me up, gets my mind out of the way.)

3. The Lord speaks His thoughts through His Spirit into my heart. (I Cor. 2:9,10)

4. His Spirit is in union with my spirit. (I Cor. 6:17)

5. Unmeditated thoughts and impressions flow, from Holy Spirit to my spirit, going directly to my mind where they are registered.

6. My mind's activity now is partially taken up with writing down the thoughts (impressions). This keeps me from wandering off, and stimulates my faith and obedience as I review what He has spoken. I can write freely at this time, knowing I will test it later.

7. When desiring God to speak, I no longer look and listen outwardly into the cosmos, but inwardly into my spirit.

8. While momentarily pausing for a new thought or the right word to come forth in the sentience I am writing, my mind tends to easily get involved in meditation on that thought. Instead, I send it back to focus on Jesus. One's own thoughts can easily rush ahead of the Spirit, resulting in impurity. As I wait for a moment, focused on Him, He places the "right" word or thought into my heart.

A Philosophical Backdrop for Experiencing Spiritual Intimacy

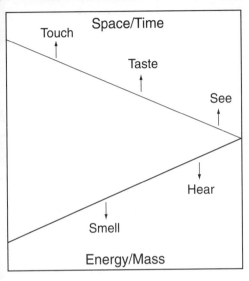

ONE WORLDVIEW
RATIONALISM

THE BOX

Spiritual World
Nonexistant or Unknowable

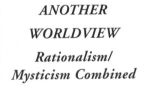

ANOTHER
WORLDVIEW
Rationalism/
Mysticism Combined

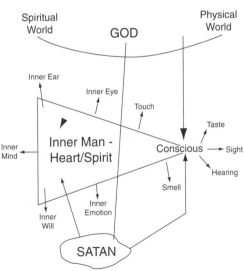

God is calling us to go beyond rational Christianity.

Rational Christianity	Spiritual Christianity
1. Code of ethics	1. The power that works within
2. Laws	2. Intimacy (Abba Father)
3. Works	3. Romance (marriage of the Bride)
4. Head knowledge	4. Illumined truth
5. Theology	5. Spirit encounter
6. External guidance	6. Bearing witness
7. Self-effort	7. Fused strength
8. Conscious level only	8. Dreams, visions, communion

The Lord spoke to me a verse of Scripture from John 5:39,40. He said to me, "Mark. You search the Scripture, because you think that in them you have eternal life; and it is these that bear witness of me; and you are unwilling to COME TO ME, THAT YOU MAY HAVE LIFE."

It was as if a sword went through me. Of course! I had idolized the Bible! In my love for Scriptures, I had made them God, rather than a Book that God had written to me about other people's experiences with Him. I had been willing to live out of the Bible rather than out of God Himself. I was pierced within as I realized that Jesus had initially spoken these words from John to the Pharisees of His day.

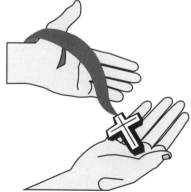